BEYOND MORTALITY

YAH-MEN

I AM THE TRUE EXPRESSION OF THE DIVINE

BANTAR-SHEY

Yah-Men: I Am The True Expression of The Divine

BANTAR-SHEY

Published by PHOENIX HEIGHTS INCORP COMPANY LIMITED, 2024.

YAH-MEN: I AM THE TRUE EXPRESSION OF THE DIVINE

First edition. April 13, 2024.

ISBN: 979-8224542765

Written by BANTAR-SHEY.

Table of Contents

Yah-Men: I Am The True Expression of The Divine............. 1

FOREWORDS 2

PREFACE... 9

ACKNOWLEDGMENT 11

CHAPTER 1 | REUNION WITH CHRIST 13

CHAPTER 2 | SPIRIT OF THE LIVING GOD............29

CHAPTER 3 | DEITY! YOUR VERY ESSENCE..........38

EUREKA | SEEK DEEPER 42

CHAPTER 5 | PRE-EXISTENCE 48

CHAPTER 6 | THE GREAT HOMICIDE 57

Also by Bantar-Shey 64

I dedicate this book to the SONS OF GOD. You all are of God. Neither your race nor ethnicity nor your religion matters. The entire COSMOS awaits your manifestation. Be of good cheer.

To my grandparents, Mr. & Mrs. Shey Emmanuel Bantar and Shey Magdalene Mafor. They have been my life's coaches.

"Man's perception of Elohim is determined by his relationship with Elohim".
LORD Elohim is Love
LORD Christ is Love
LORD Holy Spirit is Love
Love is Lord Man
Elohim's Spirit is in man making man a life-giving Spirit
Man is Elohim"
All 4 is one
- BANTAR-SHEY

FOREWORDS

"This has helped me understand better why I can only be Successful, or have the right to be Successful and I am ordained to succeed. God gave me everything of his and did not hold back. I am a God and not a demi-god. Built in his fullness and likeness.

It is a great read and I recommend every Christian to go through it."

ARREY-TEK ENOKENWA AKA G4
GOSPEL MUSICIAN CHRIST EMBASSY
CAMEROON

"I STRONGLY RECOMMEND this masterpiece to every believer in this age wherein spirits are being revived to greater dimensions all over the Cosmos.

For in it, you shall find the logos in all its veracity, and consequently be able to draw from the eternal wells of the Kenotic I Am.

What's more, at the very core of the inks that penned down this epistle, shall you find "YOU".

The Lord bless you Prophet Bantar-Shey and expose you to depths unraveled!"

REV. AKAT DAVID EBOT

YAH-MEN: I AM THE TRUE EXPRESSION OF THE DIVINE

FOUNDER OF SYNERGY OF SONS. UAE

"LOOKING AT CHAPTER 1 'The Light and Religion'

This book emphasizes the relationship between God and man.

Following the light of the Lord and not leading our children and ourselves to darkness let your light shine in great view to men.

The religion we choose and follow determines our connection with God though there are different religions. In addition, I have been touched by the topic "THE DEATH OF SIN AND DEATH" which made me understand that Sin died alongside death, Adam brought death through his sins and the Christ brought everlasting life. Therefore, here I made up my mind to disconnect myself from anything that leads me to sinning. Moreover, I know the fact that my Lord and Savior died for my Sins and everything ended at the cross and he resurrected after his death, God's love for me is unconditional, so I his child will have to be grateful, and move out of every single way that leads to sin.

Thank you for this knowledge BANTAR-SHEY"
EMILE NYUYKONGE AKA DELIGHT
YOUNG GENERATION (GOSPEL RAP GROUP)

"I STRONGLY RECOMMEND this book to anyone who seeks to rise above the ordinary.

This book gives you a sound knowledge of the creator and makes you understand and reflect on the true meaning of your Divine nature on earth.

How the writer pens down his narrative is what makes it even more interesting, following a right coherence with biblical references

If you want to understand the true meaning and essence of our promised MESSIAH and your relationship with the Divine, then this book is certainly for you."

MAKOLE EMMANUEL WELISANE

"WHAT A GREAT 'PIECE' demystifying our union with the creator, the truth made simple. A must-read for all who seek the great beyond."

B.D EYAKWE

"I HAVE PERSONALLY KNOWN Bantar-Shey as a brother who loves to search for the deep and interestingly, his concepts and depths of God get you thinking and standing on your toes. This is because they are beyond the thoughts of a normal-thinking mortal; I am telling you the truth. Moreover, I term him "Mad" sometimes because his thoughts are way beyond him. However, the fact is he brings in the depths of God that will blow your mind.

Has written an intriguing book titled "Yah-Men" which is a must-read for every individual, and I strongly recommend it. In this book Yah-Men, he brings out insights of our identity

YAH-MEN: I AM THE TRUE EXPRESSION OF THE DIVINE

in Christ and who we truly are, notwithstanding our religious backgrounds. He tells us in this book that "Christ was slain before the foundations of the Earth". Who says that and is that proven? Hahaha! (Laughing) He says this happened before the conception of time, before the New Testament. Now I know every Believer will read this and term it a "fallacy" but until you read this book thoroughly, it will be difficult for you to grasp the intelligence between the lines. Trust me; your understanding will be enlightened to some powerful revelations.

Many of us today have terrible misconceptions about Religion. However, he gives us a different standpoint about Religion that every individual should know about what it is he says. I Quote; " Religion is Peace and reconciliation' kaii!, he goes further to say Religion causes us to think about how to re-bind ourselves or reconnect us in unison with God who is more intelligent and loving" What an insight.

I could want to explain to you every detail found in this book but no. For you to grow spiritually, you will have to study, using this masterpiece as a reference. I recommend this book with all zest. Yah-Men is a blessing to Christendom and it is a must-read for everyone.

God bless you as you grab a copy and dive into the depth of the knowledge of your essence in Christ."

DANA AMIKEH (GOSPEL MUSIC MINISTER)

"I STRONGLY RECOMMEND this epistle to every believer of any and every ethnicity or spiritual background as it unifies us all as one as should be.

This magnificent piece not only helps you find "YOU" but also solidifies your knowledge of YOU within the GODHEAD.

This read demystifies the boundlessness of the Godhead and how you carry that very nature in you, opens your mind and eyes to spiritual realms and knowledge you need to be aware of!

Bantar-Shey, the author, whenever we have a deep spiritual talk, all that comes to mind is "In this dispensation, all this you carry ought to have a place in the Good Books". May Abba keep taking you deeper so you take this cosmos to where it ought to be in every dimension. Thank you for your dedication to this and all the sacrifices it had taken you to get here. I am proud of you!"

PRIDE BIH FUBE

"TRUST ME, I HAVE COMPLETED the write-up and anticipating the book release. I intend to buy a copy once it is out. This write-up is rich with the Spirit. Moreover, it took he who searched deep to unveil the wisdom penned down in this document.

God truly spoke through you and you listened!
Humanity will hear you, Sir!"

PROPHET TAMUNANG SALIFU
(FULL GOSPEL MISSION CAMEROON
DENOMINATION ELDER)

"THE SON OF GOD (CHRIST) became the Son of Man so that the Sons of Men returned to their God stature. Failing to comprehend this truth and fact, Man will keep trying to please God out of Christ and this my friends is impossible. This is so because, through Christ, the Godhead sees equality."
BRIGHTSON E. YENGONG (REV. EVANGELIST)

"THIS BOOK IS A REVELATION and a revealer of who we truly are as children of the most high. Highlighting our identity in Christ brings us to the point of consciousness of The God nature in us through the oneness we have in him. This in turn banishes any thought of failure in our lives and magnifies the consciousness that we were created only to succeed & we are of the same nature as him.

I recommend this for every believer who has been living in doubt of who they truly are."
REV. TANYU ELVIS SHEY.
CHRISTIAN MISSIONARY ASSEMBLY - CAMEROON.

"THE TRUTH REVEALED in this book is not for the average thinker. It forces you to go beyond what you have known and start asking real-life questions. It is a breath of fresh air and a moment of refreshing with every bit of revelational knowledge expressed about the divine essence of every Divine being. UNTIL CHRIST IS FORMED IN US"
NORA SAKAL

BANTAR-SHEY

FOUNDER OF PLEROMA MINISTRIES

PREFACE

There have been a lot of teachings on identity and the nature of Elohim, but the profound knowledge of the nature of God in man is what is absent and this is why this book is here to enlighten you about the very essence of the nature of man. How we were brought up and the kind of company we keep, most times hinder profound knowledge and understanding of who we are. Let us take a dive into the deep and make eureka for ourselves.

Man's perception of God is determined by his relationship with God. Man is on a daily quest to know God and gain an understanding of who He is. This quest has made man try extremely hard to know God because he is ignorant of the fact that it is not by his strength, might, or power that he can know God. Elohim in his fullness: (Abba) Father, (Imma) Mother, (Ben) Son, and (Ruach Ha-kodesh) Holy Spirit has brought illumination to our sub-conscious/minds/spirits by rightly expressing His Word (Christ), and rightly dividing Himself through His Spirit in us by the decoding of the logos (letters), giving us the truthful Rhema (uttered Word from profound revelation). It is not just the Bible, but also other materials that have been inspired by God talking about Elohim and us.

Let us face it, we are the expressed image of the God-Head and therefore called by God to steward the Earth (Atmospheric Heaven). The era in which we are is not the era of servanthood but the era of Son-ship. We are all sons of God. And we live forever because we are what God reveals we are. We are the love of the earth because the Father lives in us and as God be love and peace, and we are in Him and Him in us, we therefore are Love. Man's original nature is Love and Peace, which are like Siamese twins.

The Lord Holy Spirit is quickening our mortal bodies but the consciousness of that truth is what man is processing. The acceptance of this truth is not an easy pill to swallow, giving man more time to become a visible spirit like the resurrected Yahshua the Christ. In this book, I will be interchanging the names randomly or in most cases using just (Abba) based on our views to ease our understanding of the subject. By the Grace of Abba, I have taken out time to elaborate to us the nature of the Godhead in his full dimensions that dwells in us through the LORD Holy Spirit, which is the Spirit of Yahshua. There is one Creator though the Godhead functions in different dimensions, working accordingly in us and the cosmos, that we should rightly function in this Heaven called Earth. Let us discover this truth about our nature as we unfold this mystery. Most of the Biblical passages are from the New King James Version. This does not mean you who are reading are obligated to use it for your referencing.

ACKNOWLEDGMENT

This book would not have been a success without the help and assistance of some very important people who bought the vision and worked with me to ensure its success.

My Spiritual father & mentor, Dr. Hokage John Ndongo Ndongo is a mystique in our time, who has outrightly fashioned my thinking and taught me a lot concerning my essence in Christ.

My hero who lives in me, Grandpa Shey Emmanuel Bantar. Until infinity, I will always honor and acknowledge you. Because you wholeheartedly expressed the Divine, I became.

My Grandma, Shey Magdalene Mafor, you are my living legend and as you age, your wisdom cannot be measured as your teachings since my birth have fashioned me until date. I am honored and loved by you.

My mother, who is a great divine guardian who has nurtured me through the school of life and is still standing by me to date as one of my coaches. Mrs. Evelyne Mabaah Shey.

The founder and CEO of Omega One Entertainment and Chairman of Cameroon Film Industries (CFI), Madame Elung Brenda is one of my coaches.

BANTAR-SHEY

My Spiritual Mother Pastor Cécilia Charles and my second Spiritual Father Apostle Hilton Albert of Christ Ambassador's Ministries Saint Martin, I am grateful for your teachings through the expressions of the Christ that you both are.

To my brothers, sisters, and friends who have been with me in every step, thank you.

CHAPTER 1
REUNION WITH CHRIST

"This Consciousness is the 'only begotten Son of God,' so designated because it is the sole perfect reflection in creation of the Transcendental Absolute, Spirit or God the Father." - PARAMAHANSA YOGANANDA (Hindi Mystique)

To be joint with Christ in fellowship is a very precious gift granted to mankind after their reconciliation by the Living Christ Yahshua unto God. Union symbolizes the coming together of two people based on the kind of relationship intended to be established or one that is already established. The manner of our view towards Christ determines our relationship with Him. Some look at Him solely as Master, others as Brother, others Husband or Wife but above all, we look at Him as the Messiah (Anointed). Etymology. Christ comes from the Greek word χριστός Kristos (chrīstós), meaning, **"anointed"**. The word is derived from the Greek verb χρίω (chríō), meaning, "to anoint." In the Greek Septuagint, Christos was used to translate the Hebrew מָשִׁיחַ (Mašíaḥ, messiah), meaning "[one who is] anointed". As Christ is clinging unto the Church (US), so is a man unto his wife and the word cling means to "hold on to", in

Greek "syndéomai". The consciousness of our bond with Christ now as it was in eternity, gives us full access to the hidden and visible treasures of the Kingdom. **Isaiah 45:3.**

Let me establish something interesting that will help us understand further, what I mean by 'reunion'. Here is my reasoning on the concept, just follow and you will see. Remember that the Book of Revelations is established based on the statement written by John the Apostle, which denotes "... the Lamb slain from the foundation of the world." **Revelation 13:8.** Free your mind and kindly follow. There are some things you will read and see in the later chapters, which will give you a better understanding of what the statement means. For now, let us look at it: The verse starts with a continuation of what the previous verse talked about regarding the beast, which is a metaphorical figure, and concludes with the certainty of a particular reality we do not pay attention to. Yahshua, before time, was established and before the Earth's foundation was formed. We know that there is a foundation before a building is established, if not, nothing is built. It therefore means that Yahshua's death, burial, and resurrection had already occurred, and because of this, God said "Let there be LIGHT, and there was LIGHT" **Genesis 1:3.**

The present and the past had to manifest simultaneously because the present is the manifestation of the past. Now this is not the kind of past we know which has to deal with our memories, rather it is the past that is found in eternity and it manifests in time. If we are to apply the English Language properly, it will read "... and there is light" in the closing statement. Yes, it may seem confusing though very practical; we need to behold the texts through Divine Spiritual lenses. Yahshua was sacrificed for all mankind before the beginning we know, through the record in the Book of Genesis. Yes! Bantar-Shey what are you talking about? You are not making sense. It may be true to you reading at first glance out of curiosity but look deeper. We have existed before in spiritual form and now, we are simply manifesting what we already lived and we can decide to live better and correct the wrongs we had earlier lived till we accomplish God's will for our lives, which is knowing him as you are in all totality. So, we are being reunited with God in His fullness as we gain consciousness of who we were before the foundations of the Earth and Time as God had earlier pre-ordained, Just as Adam and Eve in the cool of the Garden, Fully God (Spiritual state of Light) and Man (Physical state of Light) and not Human. The Word "Human" to me is a degrading of my or our state of being or nature.

All things were made by Him and for Him, **Colossians 1:16,** as joint heirs with him, all things were made for our sakes **Romans 8:28.** The opening of His heart for us to belong in Him is the fullness of all Wisdom, Knowledge, Understanding, Grace, Power, Anointing, which are all components of Him in us. We need to know what or who Christ is before we can establish a solid relationship with the Divine. Many people believe Yahshua is the first incarnation of God. The question is, are we sure about that? Alternatively, do we just want to believe what the world tells us? What does the Spirit tell us? Is Christ just for the Christians only or us all? Tell you something you probably know. Christ is for all creation.

Father Richard Rohr in his book 'THE UNIVERSAL CHRIST' wrote and I quote "En Cristo" which seems to be Paul's code word for the gracious, participatory experience of salvation, the path that he so urgently wanted to share with the world. Succinctly put, mankind has never been separate from God— unless and except by its own negative choice. All of us, without exception, are living inside of a cosmic identity, already in place, that is driving and guiding us forward. We are all "En Cristo", willingly or unwillingly, happily or unhappily, consciously or unconsciously. Paul's ideology of "En Cristo" is the totality of all creation in God, with God, as God, about God embodied as one. "En Cristo" simply means "in Christ" or "in the Anointed(ing)". I agree. Looking at this book will enlighten you if you let the Holy Spirit take you through it. Personally, my experiences with the truth are mind-blowing. If I have to start telling, then it will be a long read for you, right?

Colossians 3:11 "Where there is neither Greek nor Jew, circumcision nor uncircumcision, foreigner, Scythian, slave, freeman, but Christ is all things and in all things."

The axiom made by PARAMAHANSA YOGANANDA (a Hindi Mystique) wrote, "This Consciousness is the 'only begotten Son of God,' so designated because it is the sole perfect reflection in creation of the Transcendental Absolute, Spirit or God the Father." This thus explains that believers who come to a deep understanding of truth will experience this infinite consciousness or mind called the 'only begotten son of god' It is a state of absolute reality in the experience of the creator's nature in Mankind without any fault.

THE LIGHT

LET US DATE THIS TRUTH back to the beginning as it was written in the Genesis Legend written by Moses the great Hebrew liberator. "Let there be light". This verbal expression in the beginning of Genesis reshapes our perception of Christ. Light is revealed to the cosmos so that all things created will manifest it. Light is the first incarnation of Christ, bringing the knowledge of beauty to the consciousness of all creation. This therefore means, that Christ is in all and all is in the Christ, and to the Mayans of ancient times, the Kemites (Egypt), those from Alkabulan (Africa) in general, the ancient schools of thought like the Essence and the schools in Tibet in the East, Enoch the great mystique, or Muslims, Christians, Buddhist, Hindus and all that are one under heaven. Paul the Apostle and Father Richard Rohr, myself, and others who identify with the truth I am presenting you said, and are still saying that no divisions factions, and racial segregation matter even for a second before God yet we use these misconceptions to go against the very Law of Love.

Some brothers and sisters have decided to choose the darkness over the light though they are children of God. Therefore, it is up to us to experience the Divine Light to remind them of their Divine nature, which is Christ incarnate of God. Presence is never self-generated, but always a gift from another, and faith is relational at the core. **"I am the light of the world" John 8:12 "Let your light so shine before men, that they may see your good works and glorify your Father in heaven." Matthew 5:16.** Just do it. You must be wondering what I am talking about and you are asking Bantar-Shey, what am I to do? "Shine".

RELIGION

RELIGION IS NOT A BAD word. The definition of religion in and of itself denotes peace and reconciliation. Religion does not encourage people to "stop thinking". Religion encourages people to think about how they can re-bind themselves or re-connect in unison with God who is infinitely more intelligent and loving. The problem here is the concept or motive behind each religious doctrine. We need more people to understand the correct definition of religion and the ultimate meaning of the word religion. The word religion comes from Latin and while there are a few different translations, the most prevalent roots take you back to the Latin word "Re-Ligare". "Ligare" means "to bind" or to "connect". Adding the "re" before "ligare" causes the word to mean "Re-Bind" or "Re-Connect." Now this does not mean it is by your actions. It is to show u that your actions on themselves are useless, it is by the gracious love of God, and his action of reconnecting towards us that re-connects us to him through God- the Holy Spirit. Moreover, this is why Yahshua the Christ came manifested.

All the wars, crusades, Jihads, and racism that have occurred because of the misconception of religion could have been avoided if we had the right information concerning the word or its original intent. Now our days we do not apply its authentic meaning. Some sons of God have refused to come to reason with their fellow brothers just because they are not of like religions though the blood flowing through their veins is red and not according to their physical completion. Information is very vital. I for one used to be very angry at religion until the day I finally got the right interpretation of its meaning.

In addition, this has brought the creation of many denominations (sects) and clans in the world concerning spiritual matters. Having these denominations is good, the question is, how unified are we and how peaceful and loving are we to one another in and out of these denominations? We all need a unified body under Christ. Mindsets need to be reformed from ground zero, giving us a new perspective and meaning of who and what we are. We need to stop for a while and restudy and forget what we knew before and get fresh knowledge from the LORD Holy Spirit. We need to interact more with the Divine and get to become. Knowing only does not mean anything when it is not practiced with the leading of the LORD Holy Spirit. Where is the Love, Peace, and Unity? Why hope when that which we are hoping for is within our grasp?

I am with you true and through. My elder brother and I are on a quest to become physically the "Love & Peace of Christ" as our nature depicts, Gods. Just telling people about God and our nature in Him and as Him is not enough. They need to experience that mystical side of us. Your aura needs to be high every blessed day emitting radiations of love, unity, and peace. You do not need to kill yourself to attain the level your heart desires nor sell your soul to the darkness. All you need is to believe in that consciousness concerning your nature. The LORD Holy Spirit has never left you nor left your mind. No matter the religion (re-connect) we are in, He always talks to us. Walk with Him.

Some without knowing will scream, "The church is the only place where God's house is". That is so true I tell you, though what they actually mean is "that building that we go to is the house of God", which is so wrong. **"Church"** is the (us); we being the temple as in the living house of God become the Churches. Let us look at the meaning of Church according to the Hebrew and Greek translations: By Jeff A. Benner[1], the Modern Hebrew word for a "church" is כנסייה (*k'ney'si'yah*), written as כְּנֵסִיָה with the nikkudot (vowel pointings), and can refer to the building or the organization. This word is derived from the Biblical Hebrew root word כנס (*K.N.S*, Strong's #3664) and means to "gather together."

In the Greek New Testament, the word for "church" is ἐκκλησία (*ekklesia*, Strong's #1577) and literally means a "gathering of people." In the Aramaic New Testament, the Peshitta, the Aramaic word עדה (*ey'dah*) is used and is equivalent to the Hebrew word עדה (*ey'dah*, Strong's #5712). This word is used throughout the Old Testament and is translated in various ways including; congregation, company, assembly, multitude, people, and swarm.

Moreover, two other Hebrew words can mean an "assembly," and could be translated as "church."

The Hebrew word מועד (*mo'eyd*, Strong's #4150) also means "assembly" or "congregation" and is closely related to the word עדה (*ey'dah*). Both מועד and עדה come from the two-letter parent root עד (*eyd*, Strong's #5707), which means a "witness" or "testimony." Now you understand that we are talking about us here and not a building.

---

1.   https://www.ancient-hebrew.org/jeffbenner

YAH-MEN: I AM THE TRUE EXPRESSION OF THE DIVINE

"And I heard a great voice out of heaven saying, Behold, the tabernacle of God is with men, and he will dwell with them, and they shall be his people, and God himself shall be with them, and be their God." Revelations 21:3.

With this truthful consciousness, brethren can freely fellowship together anywhere of their choosing to the glory of Abba. We need to learn how to make others feel at home no matter where we are or who we meet or interact with. Love should be your starting point of living. It is the right attitude you need in your consciousness to live each day according to the LORD Holy Spirit, owing nothing to anyone, except for your obligation to love. If you love your neighbor, you will fulfill the requirements of God's law. **Romans 13:8.** You are a God ready to forgive, gracious and merciful, slow to anger and abounding in steadfast love and walking in peace. Just to note, there is no Old or New Testament, there is only The Testament which is Christ unveiled, revealed, and expressed in us and through us in different dispensations of time.

In addition, let me give you this truth in another way **"Consciousness".** Yes, you read it right. You see when you start understanding the root meaning of words as they were derived and then you look at how they are used, you will then discover the misconceptions that have been derived and manipulatively applied to lure us out of the truth that brings us into the full manifestation of ourselves as Divine beings.

Rebinding brings one aspect to mind, a reunion of cells so that ONENESS of "Celf" can be attained. Yes celf, why use such a word which doesn't exist in the English dictionary? Well, I am simply creating the spell that will awaken your mind to the reality that you are, "a collection of cells at work to function in a particular manner which you determine". The Body's Mind, The Soul's Mind, and the Spirit's Mind must come to that fusion and acceptance of celf, making what you call self-awakened and aware. I may seem mad saying it in this manner but the definition of the word Religion is not applied and many folks just attack the misconception without having an in-depth view of the root meaning of the word. Let me submit it in this manner; anyone who understands the root meaning of words will be able to master their domain and control as they see fit. I had earlier mentioned that the different sects that exist are on a quest for God but what they do not understand is this; they all represent parts of the human body trying to attain Divine awakening individually forgetting that it is a collective effort. Just take a pip at the cosmos and there you will find your answers. Without the cells working together to build and understand the functionality of the lead cell in that organ, the organ cannot function right. This is to imply that, without the people in these various sects, the head is useless.

YAH-MEN: I AM THE TRUE EXPRESSION OF THE DIVINE

HEIRS WE ARE

HE MADE ALL THINGS and for Him; therefore as joint heirs with him, all things were made for our sakes. The opening of His heart for us to belong in Him is the fullness of all Love, Peace, Wisdom, Knowledge, Understanding, Grace, Power, and Anointing, which are all components of Him, which is He as us. He makes us whole and keeps us growing in the mystery of His God-Head nature of perfection. Man reunited with Christ is the reality of the shadow of things that were.

This brings me to the consciousness of the fact that our faith in Christ who lives in us is the presence of a powerful present growing into the perfect future (a nearer present yet manifested). We are all kingdom builders. Our nature is entitled to God. We have to implement and issue Love, Unity, and Peace (The truth of the Gospel) for all. That knowledge that Paul the Great brought to our consciousness in Philippi, births the attitude of courage to do all things "En Cristo". **Philippians 4:13**. Christ Himself which doeth them as us. Therefore, our attitudes and lifestyles need to change day in and out with the Elite one in us. He knows who we are so His aura will change you and it is not by your effort because your efforts alone are like filthy rags. God changes from glory to glory for our sakes, so that our riches in glory in Yahshua the Christ can manifest fully in the physical.

Reunion with Christ never began 2018 years ago but from the womb of eternity itself. In creation, as earlier explained we were all designed in Father's likeness to function as him. When we lost that consciousness of our identity, it initially was restored from the foundations of the earth before it was physically manifested fully 2018 years ago, though it manifested in some individuals before Yahshua appeared in the scene. That does not mean we were not in reunion with Christ no. Everyone who was born from the time of Adam was in reunion with Christ. Ideas, creativity, and all that is beautiful spring up from the depths of the Christ at work in us. That is to say, for billions of years according to the African knowledge of time, we cannot allocate time or space to Christ's existence.

Christ existed and still exists and our ancestors, the people of the old like my Ancestors of Africa, the Mayans, and the Babylonians, as many as they were, were all heirs in Christ. He knocks at the door of your mind, to give you awareness of who He is and what He has done for your sake and urges all to open up and be awakened to that consciousness. Yahshua wants you to share with him as he shares with you. It is regarded as a communion between brothers who share the love of the Spirit of God. Give Him praise, give Him honor, seek His kingdom and His Righteousness and He will feed you with all that is yours from the womb of eternity. **Revelation 3:20**

Before Christ was slain, something extraordinary happened. In the Godhead dwelt (Abba, Son, Holy Ghost & Man "His idea"), that is why all this which Adam named when he was given a manly nature and a kingdom to rule over, it was so unto God. **Genesis 2:19.** When man was brought down to earth, he thanked the LORD Holy Spirit for giving him that life he lived before time, which has permitted him to be yet again with (Abba) Father his creator. (Found in one of the seven books of Moses). Adam was God made manifest in the flesh, yet got destroyed by intoxicating his mind by himself (a problem of choice), and later on got restored and now dwelling in Christ to live yet again as God in the very kingdom given by the LORD God Almighty.

Most times, we feel we live by ourselves as in just the physical matter doing things but we cannot function with the physical matter without the very Spiritual matter in us, which is Life (LORD Holy Spirit). Adam had the LORD Holy Spirit for him to live on earth, giving him the access to be together again with his Father always as a spirit. Reunited with Christ is the abundance of spirit (life) which is God himself. That is why the Comforter (God in Spirit) had to come to make us live the abundant life that was prophesied by Christ (Anointed), which makes us eternally saved. The reason why Paul told us we are joint heirs with Christ Yahshua was an explanation of what was in eternity that is now the resurrected Christ. **Romans 8:17**

"My Bond In and With Christ – My Salvation
My Salvation in Christ – My Eternal Abundant Life
My Nature in Christ – My Personality
My Personality in Christ – I Am Christ"

My God! What I mean above is we are becoming the already expressed Christ in and out. That is, we reflect our nature through character, communication, and relationships. Just as Christ is, by His Spirit we are the same spiritually and physically. That is why the LORD Holy Spirit quickens our mortal bodies. **Romans 6:10-11.** Paul said "Christ in me the hope of all Glory" **Colossians 1:26-28**, the later Glory that all things are based on the revelations gotten, is the manifestation of the Glory of God and that is the knowledge of the bond with Christ. The knowledge of His Glory.

On August 7, 2023, my brother B.D. Eyakwe and I were engaged in a deep conversation for over 2 hours and 10 minutes, regarding our nature and God. We concluded that there is no separation when it comes to God in his fullness. What changes, is the knowledge we acquire based on our consciousness of His light. God, in the dimension or authority of the Father, Mother, Son (male and female), and Holy Spirit is one person operating differently according to the ordained dispensation of time. Preachers of old have separated the head into three based on the understanding they received. Let us look at the best or rather perfect way of beholding. We established that as God is complete in the singularity yet operational in three dimensions as we relate with him, we also are the same, without any measure. Man is a Spirit, a Soul, and a Body. Remember I mentioned earlier that the Body is the physical manifestation of the LIGHT, which implies that man cannot be separated from himself. Right now God is right here with me and right there with you at the same time.

Furthermore, if you doubt me, just look at the Living Yahshua after the resurrection (everywhere and anywhere), does it ring a bell? Yes, I bet it does. What do you think omnipresent means? That is how we or at least those with a deeper consciousness are already practicing this reality, take the Patriarch Enoch as an example, he lived this reality without even experiencing the lesser dimension of life (death). I think if I was verbal with you who is reading now, I may probably be making some sense. For you to manifest your essence in God as He is entirely, your spirit needs to reunite with your soul and body. This is what we mean, your Spirit needs to have total dominance of your soul and lead it and feed it with Divine intelligence, causing the soul to become one with the spirit, thereby causing the body to be quickened or made alive as a spirit also, reunited as one, completely in functionality as God is. Bantar-Shey you have grown bad you would say. Tell you what, if I am not crazy about expressing God, then it is not God expressed through me as me. "Infinite Creator" thank you for granting us illumination of your truth concerning you and us Amen!

***"Christ in me, I am the Glory made manifest"
–Bantar-Shey***

My very acceptance of the knowledge of my reunion with Christ is the power that reveals the attitude of Divinity that manifests through me/us by Christ in the Kingdom on the earth. As Christ is the expressed image of God, as Christ is the firstborn of all creation that makes me the second born of all creation. That is why man was given dominion over all things. That is why in him Wisdom is profitable to direct you to grow, which the LORD Holy Spirit as a son of God leads.

That is why the spirit needed the body and soul to govern the Earth and keep it with all creatures in it and also to keep his brethren as he saw his father do with his senior brother LORD the Son (Yahshua the Christ) and love all as Abba loves them right from creation.

In Paramahansa Yogananda's book entitled 'The Second Coming of Christ', he makes mention of something true and very fascinating. And I quote "In titling this work *The Second Coming of Christ*, I am not referring to a literal return of Yahshua to earth....What is necessary is for the cosmic wisdom and divine perception of Yahshua to speak again through each one's own experience and understanding of the infinite **Christ Consciousness** that was incarnate in Yahshua. That will be his true Second Coming."

CHAPTER 2

SPIRIT OF THE LIVING GOD

"The Spirit of the Living God is the Spirit of the living Yahshua the Christ without Measure"

We are all spirits and our heavenly father never gave us Himself incomplete because if He did then we are not Gods but demi-gods meaning we do not have complete power and dominion. **Genesis 1:26-28**. The complexity of the comprehension of the Logos (letters) concerning the Spirit is because of man's inability to function by the Spirit. The people of the old, that is the prophets, and the kings did receive the Spirit of the Lord but they were not fully aware of its abundance within them and thought it small upon them. It was temporal in their minds-eye, so their ways of functioning were limited, except for some particular few. All of creation has the Spirit in full measure. **Colossians 2:9-10**

"Divine perfection is precisely the ability to include what seems like imperfection". – Father Richard Rohr

The spirit with measure functions based on time, purpose, and our intellectual understanding of things occurring in and around us. The spirit without measure functions in and out of season. We are of the LORD and are complete in Him by nature, for we are not of this world. Now the (b) part of this verse makes me feel that we are yet to wait for Christ to come whereas He came already and He lives in us by the LORD Holy Spirit before time and in time.

"For the LORD Holy Spirit is the Spirit of Christ." -Rev. Akang David Ebot

The fullness of all things in God is without measure and so it is with all perfection in us operating through us by the LORD Holy Spirit who possesses us and by so speaking, the fullness of the Godhead dwells within us.

Let us face the truth of who we are and stop feeding ourselves with the lies of being slaves. We are sons of God complete in Him with no faults, as our mortal bodies are made alive while we grow in the knowledge of Him in us. Examine these references along with me:

"But to as many as did receive and welcome Him, He gave the authority (power, privilege, right) to become the children of God, that is, to those who believe in (adhere to, trust in, and rely on) His name." John 1:12

"But if the Spirit of him that raised up Yahshua from the dead dwell in you, he that raised up Christ from the dead shall also quicken your mortal bodies by his Spirit that dwelled in you." Romans 8:11

The comprehension of this verse is simple. For us to gain the light of who we truly are, who possesses us, and what is in us, we need to gain consciousness of a perfect functioning of ourselves in Christ. The reason why I said, "gain consciousness" is because we are born children of God and not made. The reason is that our salvation and nature were given long before we were born. I do not think there is someone who is 2018 years old if we are to consider after the physical death of Yahshua the Christ. Christ redeemed man then, finally, and made man conscious of the Divine nature. The process of becoming is simply gaining and growing in the knowledge of the Divine and being a practitioner of the essence.

This verse, therefore, means that our DNA is not human and will never be human as far as we are conscious or not, we are of God due to our redemption by the shed blood of our senior brother Christ Yahshua on the cross and fully operate as man. His blood now flows through our veins, making us new in His expressed image (**They are born of God).**

"Who owe their birth neither to bloods nor to the will of the flesh (that of physical impulse) nor to the will of man (the natural father), but to God. (They are born of God) John 1:13

Ok let us regard it like this, Christ has the fullness of the Godhead and we discovered above that the Spirit was given to Him without measure and now he is in us and we are no longer condemned making us complete spirits. The question is, can we operate like the way Yahshua the Christ did? Get this, yes! We can do it with all authority and boldness restored to us by Christ himself to do that which you came to earth with as a purpose and your ordained assignment right before you were born.

Remember what Christ said according to the eyewitness report given by John the Beloved.

"Then Yahshua said to them again, Peace to you! [Just] as the Father has sent me forth, so I am sending you. And having said this, He breathed on them and said to them, Receive the LORD Holy Spirit! Now having received the LORD Holy Spirit, and being led and directed by Him] if you forgive the sins of anyone, they are forgiven; if you retain the sins of anyone, they are retained." John 20:21-23,

This makes us understand what we can do as Deities in the Kingdom of God.

Never doubt for a second who/what the LORD God (Abba) has put in you, it will destabilize the consciousness of your nature/identity in Him.

Christ has given us the fullness of all things true, most importantly, what man hungers for "Power". Now you see we control this aspect in Him. Know this clearly for when you exempt Him from the equation of power, your functioning is nonsense and vain. We are the expressed image of the GODHEAD.

"There is nothing greater in this cosmos than identifying the source of all things with all benevolence in all of creation". ***Dr. John Ndongo Ndongo***

All is in the creator and the creator is in all.

YAH-MEN: I AM THE TRUE EXPRESSION OF THE DIVINE

THE LORD HOLY SPIRIT

THE LORD HOLY SPIRIT is not man and not a thing. He is a living Spirit. He has a life on His own, as did Yahshua the Christ. Matter of fact He is God in his original state (LIGHT, LIFE, and SPIRIT). Man's DNA carries the LORD Holy Spirit within him and therefore makes him a spirit by nature; this therefore makes the LORD Holy Spirit our ancestor and not Abraham. We mentioned that the Spirit of the LORD is the Spirit of Christ which signifies that He is the Spirit of the LORD God Abba Himself operating in us. We are reborn as spirits and if we can understand the concept of like begetting like, then we affirm the concept of spirit begetting spirit.

The LORD Holy Spirit knows all things and he shows us all things according to the will of the Abba (Father) which is still Him. He does not function according to our space and time for His sphere is beyond the astral and the natural. In order for man to function in that dimension, he needs to renew his mind constantly with the Truth of that dimension in the knowledge of Christ and constantly seek spiritual insight, gaining Divine intelligence into these realms.

I cannot teach you about Him for it is not my place, therefore He will show you Himself as you keep walking with Him. Walk with the LORD Holy Spirit and you will experience the spiritualized form Yahshua the Christ experienced and that of Elijah and Enoch also. Exempting Yahshua the Christ, one man outshines the rest in his walk with God and his name is Enoch. Honestly, I cannot begin to explain to you what **Genesis 5:24** did to me four years ago. I went mad in God and that was when my true Journey began. This man walked with the LORD God for three hundred years after gaining illumination for sixty-five years and not days. Folks sixty-five years he asked, sought, knocked on the LIGHT following the teachings of his fathers before him, that is from Jared to Seth to Adam and you think he was a mere man? Impossible. He became the cosmic watchman and to date, he still is, though this time as an elder in the LORD God and the Divine council. That I believe. You may have another insight on the subject but I trust the singularity of the Spirit. Do you know what it means for a man to stand as an Advocate for fallen angels? Wait you must be wondering where I am driving at right? Let me help you a little, Fallen Angels came to him and not the other way around. He was LIGHT personified to that extent (Study the Book of Enoch). I am not sure, for if you knew, you would not think to walk with God by your intellect nor strength but you would surrender your entire self for the quickening of the LORD Holy Spirit to take place in and out of you, so you enjoy your walk in His Godly dimension. I employ you to ponder in and with the LORD Holy Spirit on this.

In addition, God in His Peace has shown me things I can't even begin to describe to you, nor explain to you, but one thing He said to me three years ago in one of our conversations goes thus, **"many are the infirmities of the righteous but the knowledge of the Godly will uplift them"** and it is this year in August 2021 that I came to understand its meaning through the teaching of the LORD Holy Spirit in the gathering of the brethren in sweet fellowship with him. This statement in itself means this, those who have come to understand that they are the (in) Spirit and yet walk in the body, by portraying Godly righteousness, the knowledge of the LORD God Almighty in His fullness, walking with the Lord Holy Spirit will teach you about yourself in God and bring you to that consciousness where you will see yourself and experience the Godliness the LORD God and the Father gave you.

Never forget this, converse with your Father through His Spirit. Speak in tongues and forget yourself in the LORD Holy Spirit. This is not for Christians but it is for all men. For the LORD Holy Spirit dwells within you as His temple, forget yourself, your sense of trying to belong to a particular order, forget the nature of your color for it does not matter at all. For I love you just the way you are in the LORD Holy Spirit. So, let Him change you for Himself. Though your heart is desperately wicked, only He will change you through His own heart in His love and peace. I am the beloved of God and so are you.

Furthermore, as I walk with Him, I give up so He and He alone express Himself in me as he permits me to express Him outwardly and to the entire cosmos. There was once a time I said to a brother of mine **"No matter what happens I cannot die for in God through the LORD Holy Spirit, I AM because I love God and the Father yet not through my love but that of the Father".** Brethren with this consciousness, you cannot be sick though it does not permit you to neglect medicine for your doctor is from God. Look, things are happening now that The Creator did reveal many years ago and I am in the manifestation of them.

The Inner Mind

WE BELIEVE WE KNOW the things we need to know but those things are far deeper and more complex than we imagine. Stop thinking and start seeing so you discover how it all spins around. "You think you become". This is a product of your behavior, your upbringing, and the environment you find yourself. Though pure in heart as a lamp, deadly as a lion, and fierce as a bear, with the might as a God, you need to think about the construction and creation of a new time for all to live in peace.

You discover you know things that are not even in your head but engraved from the depth of your spirit and that is all you need to know. This is intuition. I see in myself like a movie in plain sight yet my spirit troubles me, for what I see around me physically is far more destructive to me. The men of my world have sat and decided to extinguish Love, Peace, and Unity with evil as they have given their minds to vain and maleficent things beyond their comprehension. Oh! Man, when will thou adhere to the truth of Him who never dies and whose existence is in you? I die each day in thoughts and actions living yet again in He who resurrected me into His Light with all benevolence of His Divine nature.

Everything about this concept makes man feel superior to the other; the only issue here is the ability to differentiate between a Sage and a wise man. Most times, we regard ourselves as wise men based on our lesser consciousness, which is what man calls "human intellectual knowledge" and the manner in which we regard things and situations in relation to us and those around us. In most cases, we become wise for selfish reasons but a Sage is regarded as Divine. Profound wisdom is that which comes directly from the LIGHT of the LORD Holy Spirit, which is the Spirit of Yahshua the Christ.

Imagine your world ruled by sages, everything going excellently well and in order and people's lives rightly built in the knowledge and the wisdom of the LORD God. Wisdom is the Spirit and Wisdom is Christ. Christ is within us permanently and not temporally, that is the difference between some of the people of old and us of the now. We are the Sages of the World because the God of Wisdom that reflects in Christ reigns in us. Wisdom rightly divides truth to our understanding and rightly directs us or leads us into all things and brings us success.

"If the ax is dull,

And does not sharpen the edge,

Then he must use more strength;

But wisdom brings success"

Ecclesiastics 10:10

You are the success of God's finished work.

CHAPTER 3

DEITY! YOUR VERY ESSENCE

"*Man has attributed too many misconceptions in the decoding of the truth through that which is written of Him*" -*Bantar-Shey*

The world today knows those who are believers in the Gospel of Christ as **"Christians".** This appellation is very powerful and unique. This is very true according to the definition of the word. "Adherents of Christianity", which is categorized as a religion amongst others. Others define the term "Christians" as "followers of Christ". Now the big question. Was this term given by God or by man? It boils down to the misconception of the Deity in physical morphology.

"Then Barnabas went on to Tarsus to look for Saul. When he found him, he brought him back to Antioch. Both of them stayed there with the church for a full year, teaching large crowds of people. (It was at Antioch that believers were first called Christians)" Acts 11:26

"Christians" is man's appellation for the believers of Christ Yahshua our Lord and senior brother and his gospel. The people have taken it upon themselves to be called as such because it was pleasant to them in meaning and it gave them a sense of belonging. They decided to use (adopt) it as their name for them to better relate with Christ and for society to get the picture of their belief.

SAINTS

WHILE THE ENGLISH WORD *saint* originated in Christianity, historians of religion[1] now use the appellation "in a more general way to refer to the state of special holiness that many religions attribute to certain people". Religious organizations have different meanings; Jewish (tzadik), Islamic (walī), Hindu (rishi[2] or Sikh guru[3]), Shintoist (kami[4]), and Buddhist (arhat or bodhisattva[5]) also referred to as saints. You therefore see that it appears in all the various schools of thought (religious organizations) though in different appellations.

We are not Christians because we function not by sight but by Spirit. For we are all Saints in the likeness of the Godhead. The Christians are confused for they hear too much of man's voice and not that of the LORD Holy Spirit. How? Funny right Follow. They believe their future is in the hands or the tongues of those who hold Spiritual gifts from Christ known as Ministerial Offices.

They rush to many "church" organizations to listen to what they have to say concerning them, especially those who look for prophets. The Divine is not soothsaying, neither is it sorcery.

1. https://en.wikipedia.org/wiki/History_of_religion

2. https://en.wikipedia.org/wiki/Rishi

3. https://en.wikipedia.org/wiki/Guru

4. https://en.wikipedia.org/wiki/Kami

5. https://en.wikipedia.org/wiki/Bodhisattva

The Divine is the purest of nature. Our "KI", "AURA", or "CHAKRA" is energy in its purest form from both the natural and spiritual sources of life, which is the LORD God. We are boundless and not controlled by what we know but by what is revealed by the LORD Holy Spirit. What we regard as a "Church" is a building, which is wrong. We the Saints are the Church; Christ is married to us and not the building. Well, we had earlier addressed this part in the chapter above. Let me just leave this part here; Paul called us "New Creatures" **2 Corinthians 5:17**. In the last days of the month of July, 2023 I was listening to Apostle Michael Orokpo on YouTube and he said something that changed my view on our identity. When the vibrations of the words "New Creation" sounded within me, I thought to myself the depth of the words. This is what it actually means; to the physical realm, we are the unknowns, alienated from what seems to be normal. That highest state of consciousness that Godly and nothing less, surpassing and having dominance over all things living and dead. In the spiritual world, we regain our status as the ones in the council of the Godhead, 100% LIGHT. As it is above, so it is below, "your kingdom come, thy will be done on earth as it is in Heaven". **Matthew 6:10.** We are God's will made manifest in Heaven as it is on Earth.

"They do not even make a category for my allegory" – Lecrae (Misconceptions)

YAH-MEN: I AM THE TRUE EXPRESSION OF THE DIVINE

THE CHURCH

THE CHURCH IS YOU AND I as I mentioned earlier. The cathedrals, basilica's synagogues, are all fellowship centers for the churches to gather. The Church is a complete living being fully in Christ and growing in the consciousness of the knowledge of the LORD God. We are the unifiers, peacemakers, and lovers of all creation embodied in Christ. People go to these organizations and call them church though that is not what it ought to be. Divine law is not as complex as organizational law yet it is easy to master because it welcomes all within without any exception. We do not need to fight each other anymore for it is pointless. We are one in God and we need to learn from one another without insulting. Stop rejecting the witness your spirit is baring, accept it, and see beyond denominations and organizations.

Embrace your identity without fear and live with its consciousness living in peace with all of creation. This is my gift to you. Namaste!

EUREKA

SEEK DEEPER

BEFORE THE FOUNDATIONS OF THE COSMOS **Where was man when God laid the foundation stone of the Earth?**

I understand that by now you have come to the end of the book but this particular topic never ends Matter of fact you may even have another masterpiece that is in line with this one or maybe call me so we can continue in the telling of Him. Before we continue, let us define some terms;

Foundation

According to Merriam-Webster's dictionary, it means a basis (such as a tenet, principle, or axiom) upon which something stands or is supported.

In addition, it is also defined as an underlying base or support, *especially*: the whole masonry substructure of a building.

It can also be defined as a body or ground upon which something is built up or overlaid.

Finally, it is also defined as a cosmetic usually used as a base for makeup.

Now according to the English dictionary, it is defined as the act of founding, fixing, establishing, or beginning to erect.

Moreover, they did not end there. They also defined it as that upon which anything is founded; that on which anything stands, and by which it is supported, the lowest and supporting layer of a superstructure.

COSMOS

THE ENGLISH LANGUAGE dictionary defines it as the Universe and also defines it as a harmonious whole.

Merriam-Webster then defines it as an orderly harmonious systematic universe and also defines it as a complex orderly self-inclusive system

Come let us use the cosmetic definition to look into what I am actually expressing in these texts.

YAHWH/ELOHIM/ YAHSHUA/GOD in the fullness of Deity void of gender yet LIGHT and WORD is the very cosmetic position in himself before of the entire cosmos which is the makeup was included and the beauty that exploded is the Heavenly bodies and us Man. YASHUA is the wisdom before time began. Now that you follow, let us continue...

Man in the original concept had not been physically manifested. God's idea of creating man as and like Him was not established yet. Matter of fact God made His idea come to light when the foundations of the cosmos were established. When God was in Himself operating in all His dimensions without separation as we think He did, He saw the entire cosmos as Himself. He made all cosmic realities in multi-dimensional verses as He is. He saw the entire cosmos as Himself and then decided to make Man. In one of my earlier writings, I saw based on what I heard and now that I see, it is a totally different experience altogether. All that is seen from this angle of mine which is the angle of Infinity and Eternal LIGHT, I cannot function the same. Please bear with me because I can only tell you what I experienced. In this experience, everything born of GOD's Eternal LIGHT is beautiful.

Furthermore, something interesting hits my mind when I look at the particular question GOD asks Job. Moreover, by this, I am here to tell you that, Man was not in the DIVINE counsel before creation and before his physical manifestation. The womb of eternity had the celestials the stars, the Angels. Elders were not yet revealed as at yet. Well, until I am exposed to more concerning the elders I will not tell you about them any further

According to the revelation John the Apostle had on the island of Patmos, Christ as in, God's Christ was sacrificed before the foundation and cornerstone of the cosmos was laid. **John 17:5, 11, 24-26.** This period of existence was still not in any time-space. The womb of God still concealed this reality. The Christ was only known to God by himself, not even the Angels had a clue. Before Man pre-existed, He sacrificed Himself and because of His blood, He then decided to think Man into existence to live according to His will and not Man's will. It is true that events preceding the fall of one of the Kerubims/ Cherubims and the fall of Man had taken place before it physically manifested. I am of the opinion that this only played out after God sacrificed himself.

Note, He knew the man worthy enough to take His stead and manifest this reality that was but did not expose his identity then.

YAH-MEN: I AM THE TRUE EXPRESSION OF THE DIVINE

Now to conclude this question, do not freak out about what I am telling you though it is the truth. The secrets of the cosmos are hidden in the earth's foundation, these same secrets had to be infused or merged to/with Man physically through the soil Mother, which has God's essence, and also through the breath Spirit, which is God, and the Father, which is the spiritually, for him to fully manifest YAHWH.

Dr. Gregg Braden once said in an interview and one of his interviews, "Every ancient alphabet, has always from day one had several mysterious numbers associated with the letter. The study of that code is called 'Gematria'. The atomic mass of the elements are the numbers that equate to the mysterious letters in the ancient alphabet. What that means is, when you look at Man's DNA, the numbers that equate to those become one, five, six, and three, which literally reads, literal 'GOD ETERNAL WITHIN THE BODY'. It is in Hebrew, Aramaic, and Sanskrit, which are three of the root languages..." This is someone who has devoted himself to finding the truth about who we are and to make us understand that he denied any limitation and went both spiritually and scientifically just to prove to us that GOD is in us and through Yahshua we see better.

Furthermore, there are books I want to encourage you all to read, books as (Changed into His Likeness) by Watchman Nee, (Man as God Intended) by James A. Fowler, (The Great Dance) by C. Baxter Kruger, (The Universal Christ) by Father Richard Rhor, (The GOD CODE) by Gregg Braden, amongst many others. Some of them are old and you may think outdated, but when they wrote, they were way ahead of their time. Let us feel alive in the truth we confess and in the eternal life we are living. It takes courage from the Spirit of GOD to come out strong in the telling of the good news that Yahshua had exposed, and is still exposing us too. Pen it down and make it public, so that those who are in the same mind as you can benefit and tell others too.

Who determined the measure of the earth? In addition, who stretched the measuring line upon it?

The earth is/was measured according to God's eternal space. This space knows no boundaries nor has any limits. Everything calculated by man is a lie. Those who gave a calculation did not seek God's will and counsel before allocating dimensions to it. Apostle Paul and the Prophet Isaiah knew this, and that is why they said "...A world without end" **Ephesians 3:21**, and **Isaiah 45:17.** Because the earth is part of the cosmos and the cosmos is part of God, it changes from Glory to Glory as God is manifested also from Glory to Glory without an end. Man's corrupt nature has brought calamity upon himself because greed and wickedness have once again plagued their heart like an incurable disease.

Upon what was, the foundations of it fastened. Who laid the cornerstone?

God Himself in God fastened the foundations of God's earth. God's essence holds and fastens the earth beyond any measure. In truth, God's LIGHT alone laid the cornerstone.

Note, from the time man's conception into physical matter, he couldn't command his morning because God did that form and caused the dawn to know its place so that man would enjoy communion with Him. In addition, He also did it for the rest of the earth to experience LIGHT in full measure and shake of wickedness that hides in the dawn (darkness).

YAH-MEN: I AM THE TRUE EXPRESSION OF THE DIVINE

Now to conclude this truth, o! Well, I cannot arrive at any conclusion because God's eternal truth has no end. As I said before, I know you who are reading this, are bearing witness and I encourage you to write also. Join me let us tell more about the Godhead and Us. It is your turn.

[To be continued...]

CHAPTER 5
PRE-EXISTENCE

"Know thyself and thou shalt know the universe and God" – KRS-ONE

We in all our might and knowledge and in all our greatness with all (human intellect) which has been earlier explained in the previous chapters, which off course is of a lower consciousness, feel wiser than most or greater than some, giving us an image of superiority, yet some exercise this feeling the wrong way and others the right way. Many years have passed, billions in their number of our existence, and still, many years will come and pass, and some things that we have gained experience in and known and still grow in the knowledge of the Godhead, will be revisited. Some of us will be long gone and others will still be alive walking paths they choose or ordained for them before time. Have you ever wondered who you are? What you are? Whose you are? What you will become? I ask myself these questions daily and each time I ponder on them, my mind is drawn towards the Heavens. Answers are what I seek and when I stay in that atmosphere I turn to discover revelations that are very vital and intense and extremely sensitive to the point where I freak out in myself. In this book, we see beyond what we have been told or taught over time.

YAH-MEN: I AM THE TRUE EXPRESSION OF THE DIVINE

While reading this bear with me that you may be in good disagreement because it will push you to study further to gain knowledge, though I don't really care if you disagree because I am apt to learn what Father is teaching you too. All I need you to do is to listen with your mind and see for yourself with your spirit in the LORD Holy Spirit what I speak. You may also have something extra to add to what I say because Father reveals to us in different capacities based on our relationship with him and based on our hunger to know him more. Do not forget that a Father passes down knowledge to he who is ready to adhere.

The "I AM" concept that I reveal in this manuscript consists of you and the Godhead in fullness. Let me take you back into Eternity, where our journey began. The LORD God in his fullness saw beauty in all things and needed a part of Himself to rule over all that which he/she had named beautiful. Note: God is void of gender and because of our understanding and knowledge of what is written concerning God and us, it is safe to certify that God is both male and female because he made us as per the Divine nature "...in the image of God made he him male and female". Now, based on two masculine words (he and him), the writers or translators saw only the Father figure of God and not both Father and Mother.

Furthermore, this has caused issues because, in their understanding at the time, the female is not superior to the male, though when we cross-examine as per the Genesis saga, the female plays a major role in the male, to help the male fulfill God's will. It is true that Christ's incarnation was male but his teachings and that which Paul the Apostle tells is that there is no gender but only Spirit in Christ Yahshua **Galatians 3:28,** which is our true form, as Yahshua the Christ resurrected. The Angels in their existence were in charge of things in all the cosmos and they served, for watching over all things. Phanuel/Uriel, Gabriel, Michael, and Raphael, all Arch Angels, watching over all of the cosmic universes **1Enoch 40:9,** and as mighty as they are, they never knew the plan of the creator. The funny thing is, they all were awestruck by the change initiated by the creator. Could they have known about the plan before its manifestation or did it take them by surprise? Yes, they did not see it coming. God created all things and all beings in the cosmic universe, though Genesis starts in a partial way. I believe some information was cut off from what Moses had as a record.

In addition, in the year 2020, on a Saturday, I was listening to Prophet Uebert Angel, and he was talking about "Before Adam" What he mentioned in that message drew me into Eternity and I began seeing what he was talking about, and beyond with the help of the LORD Holy Spirit. He said that there were created beings who lived on the earth and they were men though these men did exist, they were not in the image of God. Interesting I said. He used the creation experience in Genesis to bring to light his point and it could be frightening when you ponder on it. Mankind was whipped off the face of the earth with a great flood, eliminating the wickedness and bile that grew in their hearts.

Remember that this was about the time when humans existed, they were not in the likeness and image of God. They existed to serve God but never really did. Remember that there was a light bringer to this world at that time until all was destroyed and recreation began all over again. This time around God made Man as He is. Christ (God) manifested the light to kick away the darkness so that recreation can take place. Genesis makes us believe that the Spirit of the LORD God moved over the deep. Where was this water from? What I just wrote was just to make you see where I am going with the message and why I am sharing it with you. It is safe for us to have such discourse. We need to gain enlightenment through the Spirit of God on such matters.

The LORD God therefore removed from himself God which we came to know as LORD Son (Christ) and he went ahead to remove from Christ God (LORD Holy Spirit) and when they had created the Angels and the cosmic universe, they saw the beauty of themselves manifesting everywhere without pain and suffering. It was full of love and peace. Remember, time holds no bounds here for the physical manifestation had not yet happened. God did not end there for he knew that when the physical manifestation of things takes shape, he would not be able to move out of the heavens in his form to reign over it all. An idea came to him and he called the other two in a council meeting and spelled it out to them, saying Let us make man in our own image" **Genesis 1:26,** and like I said earlier man did exist but they were not in His image.

This wonderful idea came into full manifestation from its moment of conception among the members of the council, this image joined the council of God, and the Godhead was thus complete. The image was not as powerful physically as the other beings but as Moses wrote, all of the dominion was bestowed to him and when we examine profoundly the writings, we see that "He made He Him male and Female" **Vs 27.**

Moreover, I used to wonder why women were like us, forgetting that we were one in the same being. **Ephesians 1:4.**Authority, boldness, power, sound mind, dominion, and the fullness of all things were given to the image and this image is God (God-Man). Before I came to this conclusion in recent times of August 2021, three years ago I had a conversation with Father, asking Him this question "What is the fullness of God?" (Laughing). Yes, it is funny asking the LORD God the question in that manner yet it was important for me to know. Father in His love and peace for me said "The fullness of the God-Head and the fullness of Nature" but my understanding at that time was still low and I wrote "The fullness of the God-Head, the fullness of the Man-Head and the fullness of Nature". Now, I have gained knowledge of the answer based on my intimacy with Father. The fullness of the Godhead is God in his four forms (God the Father, God the Son, God the Holy Spirit, and God the Man 'male and female'). This knowledge will never leave my spirit until I transcend and I will forever tell the world about it and nothing is stopping me. **Romans 1:16**

This is an evolution of my relationship with God and the consciousness of Him as me. Many people in the world refuse this truth, though some are awakened to a very high degree of knowledge of themselves as God. In recent years people like Sage Satguru, Dr. Deepak Chopra, Lady Opra, Dr. Gregg Braden, Keanu Reeves, Morgan Freeman, Dr. Joe Dispenza, Pst. Chris Oyakilome, Bishop TD Jakes, Prophet Uebert Angel, Dr. John Dongo, Brother Rev. N.N Wilson, Apostle Michael Orkpo, Minister Theophilus Sunday, Pastor Victoria Orenze, Bishop Ondua, Prophet Tichah Kenneth, Prophet Eyakwe, Pastor Sonia Laure, and many others share this same message which I share with you today and we are many, carrying this message across the world. All sons of God awakened and some are hiding fearing for their lives because those who have adhered to the misconception of religion have made it their mission to hinder the truth from coming out because it will interfere with their businesses and their deceptions will be exposed. Listen to me; do not be afraid anymore for when you open your mouth to speak it is no longer you speaking and as you keep walking with Him LORD Holy Spirit, His wisdom is present to guide you.

WHAT HAPPENED TO LUCI

WHO IS THE LUCI THAT everyone talks about and we are so scared of, forgetting that Yahshua the Christ defeated the entity or prince? Do not worry; we will discuss more in the following sentences. First, let us look at the name Lucifer; In the Book of Isaiah[1], chapter 14[2], the king of Babylon[3] is condemned in a prophetic vision[4] by the prophet Isaiah[5] and is called הֵילֵל בֶּן-שָׁחַר (*Helel ben Shachar*[6], Hebrew[7] for "shining one, son of the morning"), who is addressed as הילל בן שחר (*Hêlêl ben Šāḥar*). The title *"Hêlêl ben Šāḥar"* refers to the planet Venus[8] as the morning star, and that is how the Hebrew word is usually interpreted.

The Hebrew word transliterated as *Hêlêl* or *Heylel*, occurs only once in the Hebrew Bible[9]. The Septuagint[10] renders הֵילֵל in Greek[11] as Ἐωσφόρος (*heōsphoros*), "bringer of dawn", and the Ancient Greek[12] name for the morning star. Similarly, the

---

1. https://en.wikipedia.org/wiki/Book_of_Isaiah

2. https://en.wikipedia.org/wiki/Isaiah_14

3. https://en.wikipedia.org/wiki/Neo-Babylonian_Empire

4. https://en.wikipedia.org/wiki/Prophecy

5. https://en.wikipedia.org/wiki/Isaiah

6. *https://en.wikipedia.org/wiki/Shahar_(god)*

7. https://en.wikipedia.org/wiki/Hebrew_language

8. https://en.wikipedia.org/wiki/Venus

9. https://en.wikipedia.org/wiki/Hebrew_Bible

10. https://en.wikipedia.org/wiki/Septuagint

11. https://en.wikipedia.org/wiki/Greek_language

12. https://en.wikipedia.org/wiki/Ancient_Greek

YAH-MEN: I AM THE TRUE EXPRESSION OF THE DIVINE

Vulgate[13] renders הֵילֵל in Latin[14] as *Lucifer*, the name in that language for the morning star. According to the King James Bible[15]-based Strong's Concordance[16], the original Hebrew word means "shining one, light-bearer", and the English translation given in the King James text is the Latin name for the planet Venus, "Lucifer", as it was already in the Wycliffe Bible[17].

However, the translation of הֵילֵל as "Lucifer" has been abandoned in modern English translations of Isaiah 14:12. Present-day translations render הֵילֵל as "morning star" Now you know what the Prophet Isaiah meant when he was attributing the king of Babylon to the fallen Prince

After man appeared, there was tension in the Heavens. Man was given free will and apart from the other three; he exercised his free will in a just manner. This statement "Who is man that you are mindful of" is a mystery the angels themselves could not understand. They saw the exact image of God at work and they marveled though one amongst the archangels was not happy. I write this depending on what is written about him who defied God. There was jealousy in the heart of Lucifer and this caused him to be angry with his creator. Do not forget that Lucifer was the son of the morning; giving light to all of creation before Man appeared possessing all the essence of God the creator.

I can tell you this, the other watchers warned him but he did not listen. I may sound crazy but u have to follow me until the end of this. We are all aware of the coup d'état in the heavens,

13.   https://en.wikipedia.org/wiki/Vulgate

14.   https://en.wikipedia.org/wiki/Latin

15.   https://en.wikipedia.org/wiki/King_James_Bible

16.   https://en.wikipedia.org/wiki/Strong's_Concordance

17.   https://en.wikipedia.org/wiki/Wycliffe_Bible

though that is not my point. My point is Man in the fullness of God saw this rebellion and took action and the action he took was "Yes and Ahmein". Know this now anything that starts with the mentioning of "I" or "I AM" or "I WILL" is the creative aspect of God. The "I AM" is God in his totality and so therefore, with this consciousness man took action. He passed judgment on Lucifer.

Do you see now who you actually are? I in recent times came to understand that whatsoever I am experiencing now is what I have experienced before and written and I am reliving it again in this time space through memory. Well, what do I know? It is just my experience and you may share the same opinion or have a different opinion. Just listen to the LORD Holy Spirit, He will guide you in all things and show you all things, which are, which was, and which are to come. The manner in which I see things are very different from what I call normal. It comes to me as images or like a movie and I turn to feel the occurrences in myself. I understand that what I have written above may be a shocker to you but that is that and I cannot change it. From your experiences, you will discover these truths within yourself and you will recall the message of mine. I am not the author, Yahshua the Christ is. I write this to you, yet not I but Christ that writes.

CHAPTER 6
THE GREAT HOMICIDE

"**L**ife ain't been the same since death died" - KB

What a world we live in. In this world, there are people who refuse to accept certain truths and others who embrace it wholeheartedly and there are others who are just in the middle of everything. Now here comes the big question "is God with them all or is he with some? Well, we can only know if we seek knowledge. If you do remember, earlier in this book I told you that I could not teach you God because you can only gain experience in the knowledge of him. I am here to establish to you your origin in God and to make you see yourself through all the circumstances or scenarios presented. What if God never took the liberty of His free will to kill himself for our sake, what could have happened to us? Trust me we could have stayed in the law and that darkness could have ended up faster and it would take us much more time in the spirit realm to gain awakening.

Look at it this way, God came in the form of Adam and ended the Adamic curse of a forgotten identity to usher us back into the light of ourselves in Him. Yahshua' birth is still God being born in human form as he created before time to end the confused state of mind man inflicted on himself. Note that the Bible is filled with lots of parables and metaphors and at times, we think that it happened exactly as it was written though it may have been the inverse or in another form. God the almighty in his greatness as King, as creator and Father came down to the lowest form of himself yet with full power and authority to end sin. Sin and not sins is the absence of one's consciousness of his identity as a God in the cosmos.

Moreover, Many Gospel ministers preach the Bible only in its surface meaning, not the deep meaning of what was written, and they turn to fear to say this truth without compromise. Check this out; before the earth or the cosmos took physical form, God committed suicide. Please do not be scared it is the hard truth. We keep on separating Yahshua from GOD as the son who died though in reality, He is God. We established earlier that the Godhead comprises God the Father, God the Son, God the Holy Spirit, and God the Man (male and female) and so with this consciousness God in the Man form came to fulfill that which he had already executed in infinity. Man could not stand to bare the truth about himself being God so he took it upon himself to riot against himself this time around and little did he know that mercy will be shown. Look at it this way, one is in everything and everything is in one. Therefore, God in his lesser form existing without the consciousness of himself of God, committed homicide and this murderous image was forgiven and restored to his former glory, without their opinion being asked. Just look at that... It is indeed mind blowing.

Who could have thought that there could have ever been a great homicide within the council of Gods just to restore one of its members into office? I mean if it were in our human concept that is mad. God became sin and death to eradicate them from this cosmic universe, just to restore Man to his former glory.

YAH-MEN: I AM THE TRUE EXPRESSION OF THE DIVINE

Since then life has not been the same since death died. Therefore, I tell you this day, it was all worth it. From the betrayal to the homicide, it was all worth it. **Revelation 13:8 and 1 Peter 1:19,-22.** This was all initiated before the cosmos came into formation and we did not know it would turn out to be this way. We are Gods and no matter how people put it, we remain that way. One with God, in Him and as Him.

THE DEATH OF SIN AND DEATH

SIN DIED ALONGSIDE death, please do not forget, the first Adam brought death through his sin and the second Adam brought life everlasting. Paul in his letter to the Romans spelled it out clearly, **Rom 5:17** "For if by one man's offense death reigned by one; much more they which receive abundance of grace and of the gift of righteousness shall reign in life by one". When you read further right up to **v21**, you will see that Paul was not blabbing, he was simply talking from the womb of the LORD Holy Spirit. You do not need to work for what is already freely given to you.

Institutions and some school of thoughts have polluted your mind, making you believe you are a sinner and cannot come before the Lord God, not knowing that what they say is indeed heresy. You cannot be a sinner while being the Holy of Holies, impossible. Remember, it was written in the earlier chapters that your body is the temple of the LORD Holy Spirit and that God no longer lives in temples built by man's hands for He is not there because man's actions made the temple he built rejected and God decided to show him His own temple which in your heart which is your body. Did God tell Solomon to build a temple for him? No but God honored his plea to dwell on certain conditions and if those conditions are broken, not by God but by man (Solomon) God is no longer there.

1Co 6:19 "What? know ye not that your body is the temple of the Holy Ghost *which is* in you, which ye have of God, and ye are not your own?

1Co 6:20 "For ye are bought with a price: therefore glorify God in your body, and in your spirit, which are God's.

Death and Sin ended at the cross and in His resurrection. His body was given up for the sin to die, his resurrection ended death, and it was once and for all. Christ made this possible for our sakes. It is by His stripes that we are healed and not by His blood, for his blood is the seal that concludes the act of His reconciliation.

Whenever you are studying any spiritual material, let the LORD Holy Spirit show you within the letters. Remember, we know in part and we prophesy in part, for do not know everything and it is only the Spirit of God that can show all things concerning the Father and you, even in prayer. **1 Corinthians 13:9, Romans 8:26.**

The last supper explains it, **Luke 22:19-20 "And he took bread, and gave thanks, and brake *it,* and gave unto them, saying, this is my body which is given for you: this do in remembrance of me." "Likewise also the cup after supper, saying, and this cup *is* the new testament in my blood, which is shed for you."**

Now Paul explains it better in his letter to the Corinthian Church, making them see the truth of the last supper. The acceptance of this act is the acceptance of the great sacrifice God made before time and in time, the fulfillment thereof later on manifested and indeed Yahshua the Christ went without food nor drink until it was accomplished. When a man says his will, it is regarded as the New Testament that must be followed by his children. This is God's testament to us his own to follow and in the remembrance of the act, which is His great sacrifice we honor his, will. Now Paul warns us not to take the last supper, which was later termed the Lord's Supper unworthily. The question here is how do we take it unworthily? When you keep on accepting sin consciousness, you dishonor the great sacrifice of the Body of God for the forgiveness of sins and the great seal by His Blood. **1 Corinthians 11:24-28**

Love and Peace to all who gain illumination through the knowledge and understanding of the LORD Holy Spirit. You are the Church. Blessed are you oh! Seekers of Truth.

Links to know more about Bantar-Shey & his Materials

HTTPS://WWW.FACEBOOK.com/
profile.php?id=100090731780769[1]

---

1. https://www.facebook.com/profile.php?id=100090731780769

Also by Bantar-Shey

MAINTAINING THE RIGHT ATTITUDE IN THE LAST MINUTE: THE ESSENCE OF LIFE

It is the unveiling of man's attitudes and temperaments that defines him and positions him when he is faced with situations in life. Life is all about action and reaction. Life's dependency is on our relationship with God Almighty and man.

ATTITUDE INTELLIGENCE VOL I:
BEYOND BEHAVIOR

BY EXAMINING THE ROLE of attitude intelligence in
various areas of life, this book offers a comprehensive guide to
understanding and improving our attitudes. From the workplace
to personal relationships, from health and wellness to achieving
goals, "Attitude Intelligence" provides practical tools and
techniques to enhance our attitude intelligence in every aspect

of life. With a focus on self-awareness, emotional intelligence, and mindset shifts, this book empowers readers to take control of their attitudes and create positive change. Whether you are seeking personal growth, professional success, or improved well-being, this book will help you unlock the power of attitude intelligence to transform your life.

Don't miss out!

Visit the website below and you can sign up to receive emails whenever BANTAR-SHEY publishes a new book. There's no charge and no obligation.

https://books2read.com/r/B-A-AZEBB-NIYAD

BOOKS 2 READ

Connecting independent readers to independent writers.

Did you love *Yah-Men: I Am The True Expression of The Divine*?
Then you should read *Attitude Intelligence Vol I*[1] by
BANTAR-SHEY!

In "Attitude Intelligence," we explore the power of attitude
and its impact on every aspect of life. This book delves into
the concept of attitude intelligence, which goes beyond mere
positivity or negativity. Attitude intelligence is about
understanding and harnessing the power of our attitudes to
shape our thoughts, emotions, and actions in a way that leads
to personal growth and success. Through practical strategies
and real-life examples, this book provides insights on how to

---

1. https://books2read.com/u/m2EglR

2. https://books2read.com/u/m2EglR

develop and cultivate a positive attitude and intelligence that can transform our relationships, careers, health, and overall well-being. By examining the role of attitude intelligence in various areas of life, this book offers a comprehensive guide to understanding and improving our attitudes. From the workplace to personal relationships, from health and wellness to achieving goals, "Attitude Intelligence" provides practical tools and techniques to enhance our attitude intelligence in every aspect of life. With a focus on self-awareness, emotional intelligence, and mindset shifts, this book empowers readers to take control of their attitudes and create positive change. Whether you are seeking personal growth, professional success, or improved well-being, his book will help you unlock the power of attitude intelligence to transform your life.

Read more at https://koji.to/@bantarshey3000.

Also by BANTAR-SHEY

Attitude
Attitude Intelligence Vol I
Intelligence de Attitude Vol I

Standalone
Yah-Men: I Am The True Expression of The Divine
Yah-Men: I Am The True Expression of The Divine

Watch for more at https://koji.to/@bantarshey3000.

About the Author

Bantar-Shey is a young Gospel Minister. He is inspired by the works of God and led by the Holy Spirit, to write this piece of revelation for you. He is a holder of a Master's degree in Marketing, a Bachelor's degree in Technology in Marketing, and a Higher National Diploma (H.N.D.) in Marketing. He also has multiple certifications in Tech, Counseling, and Sports Marketing. He is also a Scriptwriter.

Read more at https://koji.to/@bantarshey3000.

About the Publisher

A conglomerate. We are into book publishing, book distribution, book writing, scriptwriting, proofreading, translation, real estate, entertainment, marketing & more. You can contact us on our website or email